Breadcrumbs to Purpose

Discovering Who You Are and Why You Are Here

Eva Melton

Copyright © 2020 by Eva Melton

All rights reserved.

This book or any portion thereof may not be reproduced or used in any manner whatsoever without the express written permission of the publisher.

Dedication

To my parents Woodie and Ora Melton:

God knew I needed you.

Thank you for giving me a spiritual foundation that will last a lifetime.

Table of Contents

Dedication 3

Acknowledgements 6

Introduction 8

1 Purpose as Our North Star 11

2 Clearing the Runway 18

3 Breadcrumbs to Purpose 28

4 The Frame of Our Lives 37

5 As We Lay: Purpose, Sexuality & Partners 45

6 Live Until You Die 53

7 Breadcrumbs in Today's World 60

Before You Go 64

Acknowledgements

I'd like to express gratitude to some very special people. To The Firm Foundation Church family, being on this journey with you has stretched me. You were the first to hear the principles and ideas shared in this book. You listened to them Sunday after Sunday. You asked questions. You challenged me. I'm grateful to share space with you in our spiritual family.

To my writing coach, Kirk Byron Jones, thank you for believing in me. Thank you for calling out the best in me and challenging me to move beyond my comfort zone. Being coached by you - one of my favorite authors was a dream come true!

To my sister, Azzie Melton, thank you for reading each chapter along the way and laughing with me. Your perspective helped me grow in confidence and in my written expression.

To my colleagues, Geraldine Daniels and Rodney Franklin, I extend gratitude for the way you approached my manuscript. Your insight and wisdom as pastors helped me fine-tune my writing again and again.

To all who have guided others towards purpose through your writing, I salute you. I honor you. This is sacred work!

Introduction

Standing in The Sun

I'm a daddy's girl. I even have his cheekbones and borrowed his skin tone. Before beginning Head Start, I spent a lot of my days with him. At least those are the memories I choose to cherish. My dad is stout and 6'2". I remember as we would get out of the car, if the sun shined just right, I could play in his shadow as we walked. Losing mine in his was pretty fun at 3 years old. Playing in my father's shadow meant he was close enough to provide safety and security. I had nothing to fear.

I've always treasured my relationship with him even through our toughest father-daughter moments. I loved playing in his shadow. I love books today because of all the books he shared with me. My mother reminds me my personality is most like his. He and I would ride in his blue 2 door pickup truck for hours, not say one thing to each other, and that'd be just fine. We were both content with being introverted. However, one thing I never imagined I'd have in common with him is that I would be a pastor.

As a little girl, standing in his shadow was fun. As I grew older, my own shadow began to overtake the role his played in my life both physically and spiritually. Standing at 5'11", I began developing my own sense of calling and individuality. It became clear to me that his shadow could no longer protect me. The barriers and circumstances that I face as a woman in ministry are things he could not shield from me. When I made decisions in many areas of my life, I learned that the buck stopped with me. Exiting from his shadow meant I was directly in the line of sunlight. It was at this moment that I truly began to flourish and applied the spiritual principles he instilled within me.

I love the analogy of standing in my father's shadow because it's from a happy place in my heart. Over the years, I've had to step from different shadows that were not so happy places. I stepped from shadows of religious tradition that attempted to diminish my voice as a woman in ministry. I stepped from the shadows of patriarchy, which tried to limit my power to speak without seeking a man's stamp of approval as validation first. And I stepped from the shadows of people-pleasing and into my own true voice.

This book is just one expression of what it means for me to stand in the sun. Taking the spiritual principles I have learned in life and releasing them in my own voice and expression is "standing in the sun". Being able to tackle topics that will cause tension for some but bring freedom for me is my fight to "stand in the sun". I own my experiences. I own my womanhood. I thank God for my journey.

If we consistently stand in the shadows of others, we will never realize how bright we truly shine and never know who we really are as individuals. Ask God for courage to stand in the sun! I extend my hand to you and invite you to stand in the SUN with me.

As we stand in the sun together, you will gain techniques that will heighten your awareness of barriers and obstructions to your purpose – including those constructed by others and those you have constructed yourself. We'll explore all areas of your life on this journey with one goal in mind: to bring you into alignment with your divinely assigned purpose.

1

Purpose as Our North Star

Back in 2014, I relocated from Cleveland, OH back home to Birmingham, AL. I was determined to make the estimated 11 hour trip in one day. It was a Friday and a new job was waiting on me the following Monday. I packed my car the night before and started my journey at 6 am with coffee in tow. Everything was going smoothly until traffic started getting heavy before I could even exit the state. I was in Cincinnati and soon realized it wasn't just a traffic jam, there was major interstate overhaul taking place. My GPS croaked and did not recover. After sitting in traffic for almost an hour, I maneuvered and took the nearest exit to ask for directions. Although I made the trip home to my parent's house in one day, it took me almost 14 hours to do so because of a delay very early in my journey.

I had a destination in mind but was sidetracked on my journey. I recovered and got back on the path home because I stopped to gain a sense of direction. A clear sense of direction is pivotal when in route to any destination.

The abolitionist Frederick Douglas launched and produced an antislavery newspaper named the North Star. Its name was influenced by the directions given to enslaved people to follow the North Star as a clear direction on the way to freedom in the North.

Out of all the elements in the sky at night, why the North Star? The North Star is clearly visible and never a moving target. All of the elements in the sky, rotate around the North Star as it stands still. If you step outside on any night and locate the North Star, the direction you would be looking is always North.

Purpose is likened to the North Star. Purpose allows us to gauge if we are living a progressive life. If we ever lose our way, a clear sense of purpose can get us back on track. It drives out the vision for our life. It should be a target that guides our direction, the choices we make, and even the company we keep. So, if we lose our way, just as I lost my way to Birmingham, purpose will place us back on the path home.

Like the North Star, purpose should be fixated in our lives and in our plans in such a way that everything else in our lives revolves around it. Our business deals, our relationships, our friendships, etc. should revolve around purpose. Whether you've lost your way or never knew the destination, I'm happy to meet you. I'm also happy for you! Why? When we live on purpose, the game changes and we level up in so many ways!

By now, you've probably heard of the movie and book "Just Mercy" or the Equal Justice Initiative founded by the attorney

Bryan Stevenson. In "Just Mercy", Stevenson introduces us to the day his North Star was revealed to him. Although a Harvard law student, he didn't feel passion for his path. He questioned why he was enrolled as a law student and lacked passion for his classes. He eventually took an internship with an organization in the South dedicated to representing those on death row that had no lawyers or right to counsel. His adventure as a legal intern for the Southern Prisoners Defense Committee led him to a rural Georgia prison.

His conversation with Henry, a prisoner on death row, changed the trajectory of his life. While the initial topic of discussion was Henry's execution date, Stevenson and Henry were carried away in a genuine conversation about each other. It was this moment when he saw the humanity of an inmate who was on a path to execution. Henry ignited something within him and suddenly the path in law school made sense. His interaction with this condemned man ignited passion within him and confirmed his life's purpose. Until this day, Stevenson is known as the lawyer who has dedicated his career to helping the poor, the incarcerated, and the condemned.

Purpose Precedes Vision

As the year 2020 approached, there were many prophesies that 2020 would be the year of vision. I observed many churches introduce the theme of vision in their New Year's Eve services leading into 2020. That was based on the physical sight of our eyes being at its best at 20/20. I don't desire to negate the message that this year and possibly the decade will be about vision. However, I would like to reiterate that purpose precedes vision. Vision provides a plan of how we get to purpose. Purpose is the destination. Vision is the itinerary. 2020 is the year of purpose. In the years immediately following 2020, the vision will be clear because we leaned into purpose in 2020. I caution you in this season not to rush off to vision prematurely. Take time to sit with and ponder purpose.

The life coaching industry has boomed in recent years. Every time I'm on Facebook, there is a new life coach in my network or shown as a sponsored ad in my newsfeed. One can become certified and make a career in this industry. The area I see many coaches missing is purpose. The best life coaching should be centered around individual purpose for maximum impact. If purpose isn't the driving force, then we're funding someone else to help us make plans that will never manifest anything divine into our lives. What does it mean to make plans and goals for our life for a 1 year, 2 year, or 5 year plan if we don't have purpose at the center? Allow purpose to lead the way! If the seed of our purpose is within us, I believe self-discovery and remaining open for divine revelation is the key to effective life coaching.

Even the wisdom of Proverbs enlightens us:

"Many plans are in a person's mind, but it is the Lord's purpose for him that will stand." - Proverbs 19:21

This verse emphasizes that out of all the plans we make and

dreams we have, purpose will prevail. This verse also gives us a clear indication of the source of purpose--- our creator. We were created with a purpose in mind. We were not randomly crafted. Perhaps our parents did not plan our conception, but our Creator had a plan in mind for us and it still stands. It is more than we can envisage in our imagination.

Consider the words to the prophet Jeremiah in a pivotal moment of his life:

"Before I formed you in the womb I knew you [and approved of you as My chosen instrument], And before you were born I consecrated you [to Myself as My own]; I have appointed you as a prophet to the nations."

While this message was to Jeremiah in his lifetime, this message most certainly applies to you today. Let's try it.

Repeat this statement while putting your name in the blanks:

Before I formed you in the womb,_____I knew you and approved of you as My chosen instrument.

Whew!!! How'd that feel? Felt good to me!

Now this next portion will make a lot more sense once you have located purpose. Fill in the blanks.

"And before you were born I consecrated you_____to

Myself as My own I have appointed you_____as

(your purpose goes here)."
_____

What has God appointed for you in this generation? Whew! Like Jeremiah, this is a pivotal moment in your life. What if the universe has conspired with the motive of your own soul to place this book in your hands? Perhaps at this moment on your life's journey your consciousness is open and elevated for the revelation in the pages to come.

There is a reason that you are alive now reading this book at this point in history. You were created with a purpose to be carried out in this generation. Perhaps you picked up this book with this question in mind: "Why am I here?". If you did, this book was divinely inspired just for YOU!

Are you ready to take this journey of self-discovery with me? I've been sent to lead you by the light of your own North Star. Let's go!

Do know this I have prayed for you!

North Star Affirmations

As we begin this journey, take time to complete the exercise below.

1. Write each of the affirmations below on a separate notecard.
2. Every morning for the next 7 days choose one of your notecards.
3. Look in the mirror and say the affirmation 7 times.
4. Take the affirmation card with you throughout the day. Every time you see it, bring your attention and awareness back to the affirmation by repeating the affirmation again.

Affirmation 1: I was created with purpose in mind.

Affirmation 2: The divine is unfolding within me.

Affirmation 3: Within me, rests a treasure.

Affirmation 4: I am gifted.

Affirmation 5: I am focused.

Affirmation 6: I am whole.

Affirmation 7: I am in God and God is in me.

2

Clearing the Runway

"A rested spirit is a spirit with a higher propensity to hear from God." – Eva Melton

As airplanes prepare for take-off, the air traffic controller in the control tower and the pilot undergo a few precautions. One of which is ensuring no other planes or any other barriers are on the runway. To ensure the aircraft is suitable for take-off, a pilot walks around the plane before his final board for the flight. The pilot confirms with the tower that the runway is clear and the airspace is ready for the plane's ascension. Why? It is a waste of fuel and time for a plane to begin movement towards take-off when there are barriers that would impede its acceleration and ascension. It is the same with getting on the path to purpose. There are necessary evaluations that should be completed before taking off. This chapter is dedicated to the prerequisites necessary to allow a smooth take-off towards purpose.

Surrender

Think about the last two months of your life. What was your focus? Out of all the Zoom calls, meetings, hobbies and activities you engaged in, was there an overarching tug, reason or theme?

Did your life revolve around your family, job, or passion? Did it revolve around making other people happy?

Did you have too many focal points? Were you majoring in minor things? Did you feel fulfilled? Has there been a consistent path ahead in your life?

There is only one person who knows the answers to these questions: You.

If the exercise above revealed that you didn't have an overarching theme or reason for why you did what you did, the word for you today is: SURRENDER.

Surrender to what, you may ask. Surrender to the Divine unfolding within you.

Discerning our purpose does not require us to continually search externally. It's an "inward-out" unfolding, not "outward-in" approach. Some search for their purpose among the stars. Some believe they will only connect to purpose once they find their soulmate. Others believe they must travel the world and see the great philosophers and spiritual sages. All of these are an outward approach.

The seed of purpose is within us. It has always been there. If we don't nurture the seed, we stunt its growth. This issue ensues when we become attached to non-purposeful endeavors. Those attachments block the Divine unfolding within us. We nurture the seed of purpose by coming home to ourselves. This only happens when we surrender to God unfolding within us.

When we hear the words "the will of God" and "surrender", don't immediately think about sin or immoral behavior. In fact, good things can take us off course quickly. Good things can be helping our community and helping our neighbors in an area we are not purposely made to do. We can be doing "good things" that remove us from the purpose and plan of God.

During the COVID-19 pandemic, it seemed like everyone launched a livestream show or podcast. This was a great way to stay connected while physically separated. Leading up to the pandemic, I had five years of experience producing and hosting podcasts, so it was only natural that several people reached out to me for consulting and help hosting their shows. On the onset, this appeared to be a great opportunity. After talking this over with one of my friends, I was reminded of my purpose.

I'm passionate about social media, so my friend reminded me to use my passion for this medium purposefully. My purpose is in spirituality and liberation. While it would've been "good" exposure to assist and co-host podcasts with my friends, would my overall message and purpose have gotten lost in the shuffle? The answer to that question was "Yes". "Good things" and fun things may not always be purposeful for us. If engaging in the tasks zap our energy reserve to the point of us not having energy for purposeful endeavors, then we must choose better.

The key to purpose is positioning ourselves for revelation for what's already in us! Our Creator can send us messages at any time revealing what's already in us.

Let's get clear on the source of our purpose. Purpose is derived from our Creator. We don't have to be like the cartoon character "Dora the Explorer" who searches to find the answer all over the world. Those endeavors will not lead us to purpose. As we surrender to the Divine within us, we surrender to ourselves… our true selves.

The overarching purpose in our lives is to please God. We please God by operating and expressing ourselves in the way God crafted us to do. Ultimately as believers, we are to bring glory to God and to advance God's principles on earth. Once we surrender to the Divine unfolding within us, elevating God becomes easier in our day-to-day lives.

Rest

We hear clearly from the Divine when we are rested. Have you ever awakened from your sleep with the answer to a question you forgot you asked? Perhaps you were laying on the beach and received a creative spark or message that changed the course of your plans? Maybe you were a cigar aficionado on your back porch lighting a new smoke, and as the flame lit, a divine spark from God came to you.

There must be time for rest and play in our lives. A rested spirit is a spirit with a higher propensity to hear from God.

Surrender to the Divine. Surrender to rest. Surrender to play. Surrender to your true self.

If the word SURRENDER has jolted your being, then please take the time to review your unnecessary or repetitive commitments. What meetings do you attend on a consistent basis that drain you? What board positions do you hold that do not fuel you? What circle of friends do you entertain that leave you drained?

Surrender. With an accountability partner, look at your schedule and reduce busy and people-pleasing habits. We will talk more about this later, but for now, the goal is to raise your awareness around your own commitments.

Characteristics of Purpose

To get clear on purpose, we must understand these characteristics of purpose. Here are three questions we can ask ourselves below:

1. Does it please God?

2. Does it impact a collective in a positive manner?

3. Does it increase your energy level?

Let's discuss each one.

1. Does it please God?

Our purpose does not require us to harm ourselves or others. It does not require manipulation. If operating in our perceived purpose requires us to go against spiritual principles, we consciously know to be true, it is not purpose. God is the author and source of purpose and it is not God's character to contradict Herself.

The Master Teacher gave us two guides to help steer our actions:

- a. "You shall love the Lord your God with all your heart, and with all your soul, and with all your mind."
- b. "You shall love your neighbor as yourself."

Again, operating in our purpose should not violate those spiritual truths and it should not violate or abuse our neighbor.

2. Does it impact a collective in a positive manner?

While purpose was uniquely assigned to us as individuals, it is amplified in community. It is meant to be expressed in a collective. Purpose is what connects us to the larger world. If we are in our purpose, someone else should be blessed by it.

Ne-Yo expressed it another way through lyrics: "I'm a movement by myself, but I'm a force when we together. You make be better."

The greatest force is formed when we are generous in our purpose collectively.

3. Does it raise your energy?

All things are made up of energy. Humans beings carry a certain energy. Our thoughts are made up of energy. Energy carries a vibration that can be described as a low or high frequency. The optimal goal is to vibrate at a higher energy. When we are in purpose, we vibrate at a higher frequency because there is no resistance present. In purpose, our emotions are at an elevated state because we can hold space fully as our true selves, even if just for a moment.

It is this higher frequency vibration being emitted into the atmosphere of the spaces we are in and even into the universe that begins to draw to us what we need. This is what people mean when they say, "Her vibe was amazing". People purposely in higher vibrations are magnetic.

God is the creator of the entire universe. If you are operating in your purpose and co-creating with a clear vision and plan to carry out that purpose, why would God not send a signal to the universe (God's creation) to align with what you need to operate fully in purpose? If you would only believe.... BELIEVE!

There are spiritual and physical laws that undergird our efforts when we choose to live on purpose. When we live on purpose, an energy flows from us likened to a magnetic charge that goes out into the

Universe. This magnetic type of energy begins to draw the rest of God's resources to us to accomplish things that are larger than ourselves. Our "drawing" and God "sending" are synonymous.

When we live on purpose, we draw at the level we are vibrating. Without much toil, resources are provided to us. We will notice people showing up on our path with the skillsets, personality and wisdom that are complementary to ours. This is the true law of attraction.

The collaboration between one or more individuals vibrating at a high frequency can be powerful. It is pivotal for individuals drawn together to stay focused on the purpose that drew them together. In that focus, the vibrational frequency remains high, which leads to the attainment of goals, visions, and resources. The more intent the focus and the higher the frequency, the quicker the manifestation.

Seeing Our Blind Spots

Cars typically have two side mirrors, one on each side of the car. These mirrors allow the driver to see what's on both sides of the car while allowing one to keep focus on the road ahead. Occasionally, a driver needs to change lanes in order to maneuver better to the destination. If we have any driving experience, we know that at times the rearview and side mirrors are not enough. We can miss cars that are adjacent to us, but not in our peripheral. We call this area a blind spot.

In life, in order to properly access our blind spots, an accountability partner is necessary. Accountability partners have a detached view of our life and can detect things we may not see.

Throughout our time together, you will receive directives from me to engage your accountability partner to assess areas of your life. When it comes to purpose, having an accountability partner is mandatory. We all need people in our lives who will hold us accountable, help us detect our purpose, and help us get back on the path when we fall.

Occasionally, we can become emotionally attached in certain areas of our lives that we are not able see clearly. We don't see the movement of the characters in the play.

Characteristics of an Accountability Partner:

- They hold space for you in a non-judgmental way.
- They listen to you and ask the important questions.
- They point out areas of caution when they sense them.
- On your tough days, they remind you of who you are.
- They understand where you want your life to go and find great joy in you getting there. They want you to win!

Relationally, accountability partners develop in different ways. For some, an accountability partner is a trusted friend. For others, a pastor or spiritual guide holds them accountable or function in more of a mentoring relationship. When you are blessed to find this level of relational safety, be sure to honor it.

Accountability Partners

Consider each question below. For each question, list the people who meet the criteria in your life. Do not overthink. Write down whomever comes to mind. You can list more than one person in each box.

1. Who naturally holds space for you? When a person holds space, one listens to the details of your life and cares about your experiences.

2. When you go astray, who gently nudges you back on track? Nudging means this person reminds you of who you are and the goals you've set for yourself.

3. Who is the person that helps you feel safe even when you are corrected or provided with an alternative perspective? Safety is important.

3

Breadcrumbs to Purpose

"And Hansel said to Gretel, 'Let us drop these breadcrumbs so that together we find our way home'."

It is The Creator's desire that every single creation operates in its purpose. The Divine is open and available to reveal that purpose to us so that the overarching plan and purposes of God may be manifested in our lives in this lifetime.

The potential to all we could ever be is already in us. We can stop searching outside of ourselves for who we are. The quest starts within us. Finding purpose is a journey of self-discovery. It's kind of like an adventure of coming home to ourselves.

There are several ways to get to purpose. Many prophets and pastors allude to receiving some type of direct communication through an open vision that made the direction of life clear. I experienced this phenomenon in my senior year of college, which charted my way to seminary. Visions are one of God's chosen expressions of communicating to us.

Purpose is slowly unveiled as breadcrumbs that show up on our path. They can include a massive divine revelation, but smaller tidbits of revelation can also get us to the same destination. We have the choice to pick up the breadcrumb that guides us to the next step on the journey or simply chart our own way. In charting our own way, we may never find our way home to ourselves.

Let's talk about 3 different breadcrumbs that will appear on our journey:

o Life events

o Passions

o Gifts

Life Events

Do you remember the vision I was telling you about from my senior year in college? I wasn't sleeping. I was wide awake sitting in a chair in my campus apartment in Tuscaloosa, and just like that I saw myself in the future with intricate details. I will share the overarching message communicated to me. It was "go to seminary". I was bothered and frustrated by it. I was close to finishing my bachelor's in Computer Science. I wasn't even a minister. I loved teaching new member's class and helping with any form of spiritual teaching in a small group setting. From my perspective, the vision didn't match me and the direction I was headed. I knew it was a supernatural experience, so I treasured it in my heart. I told no one about it for years.

Three years later, I transferred my corporate job to Atlanta and started my first semester of seminary in the evenings. Although it took me three years to act, I knew this was a divine breadcrumb. When I started seminary, I wasn't even in ministry and I was adamant about communicating that to my advisor as he helped with class scheduling. I exclaimed "I don't need preaching classes because I'm not a preacher!" I knew if I surrendered to preaching, I would also surrender to the call on my life to pastor. So, I intentionally stunted the unfolding of God within me. My surrender was like snail mail, slow.

By picking up and following the breadcrumb that was dropped during that vision, my life was catapulted towards purpose. As life progressed, I picked up other breadcrumbs along the way. Here I am today, pastoring a church start in my hometown, and writing this book. Sometimes I think about where I would be if I hadn't shifted my life's focus to my purpose. I would likely have been leading a Fortune 500 company and breaking corporate glass ceilings. Although admirable, this thought doesn't light a fire within me.

Another example of a life event that leaves breadcrumbs are personal crises. These are moments where we endure some situation so troubling to our soul that we draw near to spirit. Some call this season the "dark night of the soul". During this season, we start searching for a deeper meaning to life. Some crises that can precede this season are divorce, death of a close loved one, major medical diagnosis, etc. In these stages we are really low vibrationally. Perhaps we experience depression for a season. In all of this darkness, for some reason we lean into spirit. As we draw nearer to spirit, we begin to understand ourselves more. James 4:8 declares, "Draw near to God and he will draw near to you." It is impossible to lean into God and not glean from Her presence.

I too, experienced a personal crisis as my 5-year marriage ended gradually through a separation and divorce. In that season of my life I really had to take it one day at a time as I came to terms privately and publicly with my divorce. Although painful, it has been one of the most transformative experiences of my life. While I don't glorify divorce, being intentional about coming out on the other side stronger and more self-aware kept me in purpose. That season was really what nurtured the pastor in me. It gave me a higher level of sensitivity for the conditions of others and what it means to hold space for others during seasons of transition.

Passions

What ignites you? What lights your fire? What topics or conditions stand out to you?

Sometimes a parent will notice the activities a child gravitates towards. Renee is a young woman that attends church with me. When Renee was a little girl, because of her attention to conditions of oppression or observation of mistreatment of certain groups, her father called her his "Little Angela Davis".

She not only saw adverse conditions. She wanted to do something about it. Expressing her disgust was not enough for her. Today, Renee works in social services helping people who typically are pushed to the margins of society.

Renee's passion, the passion to help others, had been there all along. Why? Because our breadcrumbs to purpose already exist. The capacity to all we will ever be is already buried as a hidden treasure within us. We must be willing to pick up the breadcrumb and continue the journey home.

Kobe Bryant recalls the passion ignited in him when he got his first basketball as a kid. He loved how it sounded and how it felt in his hands. He described the sound as the "sound of life and light." He describes his passion and drive as an adult "all came back to that special tap, tap, tap that I first grew infatuated with as a boy."

Passion is not always a "feel good" thing. Sometimes our passions show up in the things that unsettle us. We may not always be excited about the breadcrumbs that help us find our passion.

As I write this chapter, Australia is on fire. Animal species that are already near extinction are being set ablaze and dying. I have not given much attention to the brush fires. I heard a radio host passionate about the topic talk about what was happening to koalas. Seeing a baby koala being rescued from a fire saddened her. I could hear the disgust of her heart in the airwaves. I didn't feel as terrible about the fate of koalas in Australia, but her passion was expressed so deeply that I have taken time to Google about the brush fires and the impact on the animals in Australia.

My best friend is preparing for a garden on his property. He lit up when the eight raised garden beds were installed. When he shares his vision and plan of the different vegetables he will grow, his energy stirs me. While gardening is not my thing, as a friend, I support his vision and appreciate the passion. I'm sure I will be the benefactor of a sweet potato or two, but I also benefit from the energy he exudes when he takes part in his passion.

The more we listen and value the passions of others, we realize we are not cookie cutter. It would be a boring world if we were. God granted us each specific passions, and it is through our passions, the world goes 'round and 'round. Otherwise, we would have destroyed it, each other, and ourselves by now.

Take time to consider your passions. You may need the help of an accountability partner that knows you well. Those that know us well can notice the things that lights a fire within us.

Gifts

Passion alone won't do it.

PASSION + GIFTS combined produce the aroma of purpose.

What do I mean by this? Have you ever met someone who was passionate about singing, but was not gifted to do so?

If you could mute them, they looked like they could sing. They had the energy of a performer, but they were just not gifted in that area.

Remember this important characteristic of purpose: It should impact a collective in a positive manner. Being passionate about singing, but not gifted to sing doesn't benefit a collective. Well, unless you have the mic at karaoke. Ha!

Consider the co-worker who brags on their cooking. They can make the best cornbread dressing with the recipe passed down from their grandmother's grandmother. The company Thanksgiving potluck rolls around. There's the dressing. It looks scrumptious, but it tastes like paper! It's dry. It's sagey. Passion with no gift.

You can be passionate about things, but not gifted in them. When it comes to breadcrumbs to purpose, we should identify passions and gifts that blend together well and produce a sweet aroma to us and a collective.

Gifts are characteristics and expressions that God has given to us that are typically a strain for others to accomplish. Each of us have been given one or more gifts. Sometimes we can't sense our gifts because they come so natural to us. That's why an accountability partner is vital in this process. Your gifts are possibly a blind spot for you.

There are some who have the greatest gifts, but they don't cultivate them. You can be blessed with a beautiful voice, but only sing when it's time to perform before a crowd. A great singer practices.

If you are gifted in an area, find ways to use that gift. In what spaces can your gift be used? What charitable organization would benefit from your gift? Is there another position on your job that you could target because it's more aligned with your gifts?

There are so many opportunities. If you set the intention to use your gifts, the universe will bring them right to you!

Breadcrumb Tracking

Take a moment to answer the following questions. Afterwards, follow-up with your accountability partner and ask for insight.

1. What activity do you enjoy that meets one or both of the criteria below?

    a. It is pleasing to God.

    b. It impacts other people in a positive way.

2. What things do you do well that does not come natural to others around you? *others – your classmates, peers, co-workers, spiritual family, family, etc.

3. Consider your passions by exploring these two questions?

    a. What do you enjoy doing that no one has to influence you to do? What do you wake up early or go to bed late to accomplish?

    b. What conditions in society unsettle -you? Consider what you see on the news or on social media that upsets you.

4

The Frame of Our Lives

"I wasn't willing to sacrifice my game, but I also wasn't willing to sacrifice my family time." – Kobe Bryant

A few years ago, I purchased a Nikon DSLR camera. As an amateur photographer, I appreciate its cool features. For example, autofocus allows the lens to adjust its focus based on the items in the frame of the picture. It automatically chooses which items to focus on. The autofocus can bomb if someone or something is moving in the picture. For instance, if a dog runs by or the clouds start moving, the autofocus feature struggles to determine the focal point, which delays the shot from being captured. Majestic and candid moments are often lost simply because of too many moving objects in the frame.

Too many things or the wrong things in the frame of our lives can prevent us from determining the focal point. If we don't have the focal point, we will have trouble executing or manifesting purpose in our lives.

Of all the things in the frame of our lives, what items are our focus?

When too much is in our frame, our energy doesn't know where to go, so it spreads in any direction with no focus. In those instances, our efforts become less impactful. Without proper energy and focus, we will never manifest our desires. The goal should be to have maximum impact with the least amount of exertion of energy as possible. Operating in this manner ensures efficiency and impact.

Focus and Intention

An intention is a desire with the force of a decision behind it.

We can set intentions all day, but unless we give that intention focus, the intention reverts to simply a desire. It becomes just a wish. Focus is the energy that gives intentions the force to manifest.

Focus requires consistent attention to the things we want to see manifested in the physical realm. Manifestation is moving from "thought form" to "material form". In other words, it is moving from an intention to physical appearance in this realm. Focus is a key component of manifestation.

The key step to focusing is eliminating non-essential activities that draw in our energy. What things in the frame of our lives are negotiable?

We must determine our priorities and understand each priority consumes a certain degree of energy from us.

The things with a higher rank in priority should be done earlier in the day, if possible. Each morning upon awakening, we start with an energy reserve. Depending on the activities of our day, that energy reserve can grow or dwindle.

So, actions that aren't necessarily productive or purposeful should come after the priority items. For example, we could decrease television and social media use in the mornings until after key priorities are done.

Why? This will help us conserve energy for our higher priority items.

Who is responsible for where our energy goes? We are. We are accountable for our "yes" and our "no". The more we say "no", the more powerful our "yes" becomes.

Check out this wisdom from artist Shanequa Gay:

"As creatives, we are naturally guarded people. "No" allows us to continue in the realm of proceeding with caution and creating with freedom. Our spirits can't handle the constant pulling and tugging that saying yes to everything requires".

It's hard to see the full picture when we are in the frame. For this reason, here is another area where an accountability partner can help.

Taking on Stuff That's Not Ours

Some of us have a trait in our personality that causes us to lean into the issues of others. While this phenomenon has its perks, depending on the circumstance, it can be problematic for us to embody the feelings of others as our own. Counselors call this trait being empathic.

Judy Dyer describes an empath as a person who is highly aware of the emotions of those around them to the point of feeling those emotions themselves. Because we can feel these emotions, we typically place ourselves in the shoes of others and began to behave as if the situations were our own.

Being an empath is a blessing, but without proper boundaries it can be a pure curse. Why? Emotions are energy. If we take on the emotions of others and express them through our own vessel, we are pulling our own energy from our own obligations and priorities.

Some of us are positioned to care for others, listen, and walk with them. However, we get to set the boundaries of the time, place, and extent we do these things with people. If we are not careful, we absolve others of their own responsibilities and consequences and we are left empty and agitated.

If you are an empath, I highly urge you to increase your spiritual practice. Find rituals that help you release foreign energy and call your energy back to you. So after you are done walking with and listening to others, you can release them and their emotions and get back to your core priorities.

Some examples of spiritual practice that can help release the energy of others are journaling, prayer, mediation, yoga, reiki, or a nature walk, etc. I personally lean into prayer, meditation, and reiki as daily practices. I hike or pursue a nature walk a couple of days per week.

Keep Your Eyes on Your Own Paper

Do you have memories of taking tests in elementary school? Have you ever been ill-prepared for a test? I definitely had my moments. There were times when I was satisfied with my answer, but I would sneak and look at somebody else's paper. In one glance, I would lose all confidence in the answer I had developed and written on my own.

For example, I know 2*3 = 6, but since my neighbor had 12, I felt insecure with my 6. LOL!

It's been said that comparison is the thief of joy. It is also the thief of creativity, confidence, and self-esteem. Often, we find ourselves looking at the lives of others to see if we are getting it right. The question is this: What if what we are doing has never been done? What if we are a pioneer in the way we do what we do? In these circumstances, looking on everybody else's paper will stifle us.

Tread carefully when sharing visions and goals with other people. Since many can't see themselves living out their purpose and their vision, they will shoot us down. They conclude that "surely if I can't do it, she can't do it."

I remember when The Firm Foundation Church was first launched. It was bumpy, but ever progressing. A lot of pastors in my life started mentioning denomination. As if denominational affiliation was the secret sauce to being "a church". They wanted me to align with a denomination, which was the exact opposite of what God was saying to me.

Of course their emphasis was always on their own denomination. If the church had affiliated with a denomination early on, it would have been premature. The process of affiliation and taking on the characteristics of denomination would have been distracting. God was calling for something new, fresh, and flexible in that season. I learned to expect that conversation to come up when sharing with pastors about the church. It was up to me to set boundaries and keep my eyes on my own paper.

We must be careful of the tools others attempt to give us. They may not be suited for the vision God has given us or appropriate for this generation.

When David got ready to go up against Goliath, he had the thing he was most comfortable with to use: his sling shot. He was confident in his ability to masterfully hit targets with it.

Those who were trained in battle tried to give him tools that did not fit him. The armor and helmets provided restricted him and were not suited for his use.

I assert that Goliath would have never been slain by David if David accepted the traditional tools over his slingshot. It's important to understand what works for us because everyone will have a critique or a suggestion. Understanding our own paper will help us receive those critiques and suggestions and trash the ones that don't apply to what God has shown us.

While we must focus on our paper, we must have a _few_ trusted confidants when it comes to our purpose and vision. Look at the word I underlined in the previous sentence: <u>few</u>. When we are in purpose we will attract many people, but our inner circle must remain small. Why? So the plans we intend to execute are not thwarted by others who may not have well-meaning agendas.

I've heard this called the "The Law of Privacy," meaning what people don't know they can't touch. What people don't know, they can't attempt to tear apart. What people don't know, they can't put their energy on. As we make plans, identify our inner circle, and if need be, rotate out those who reveal they are not truly onboard for the vision.

If our vision is truly from God, understand it will be tested. Anything of God will be tested. It's not if, but when. Applying the "Law of Privacy" means we don't allow things to be tested too soon. As we build confidence with our inner circle, we will be well prepared when the season of testing will come. The season will come, but never let the potential for testing be our focus. Let our focus rest in our purpose and vision.

Keeping our eyes on our own paper will help ensure that we are not bringing items into the frame that will impede our purpose. Keep the image sharp by focusing. We can do this!

Detecting Your Barriers to Purpose

Carefully consider each question below. Afterwards, review your list with an accountability partner and gain their perspective.

1. Over the last 30 days, where did you spend your time outside of family and work obligations? Feel free to list more than one. Next, describe the energy when you finished as draining or energizing. Example:

Activity: podcasting with a neighboring pastor - Energy: energizing

2. In what areas of your life have you allowed comparison to others stifle you? In what area have you quit or slowed down because you felt it didn't measure up to someone else's work?

3. What plans are you currently making that need to apply the Law of Privacy? Who is your inner circle to assist you in formulating the vision/plan?

5

As We Lay: Purpose, Sexuality & Partners

I'm going out on a limb here, so please stay with me. This will be a purposeful discussion. If you are a Christian, you know we approach the subject of sex in a real black and white manner. If you are married, yes – go for it. It's healthy! Express yourself sexually at your highest capacity. If you are not married, it's a big red NO! You're hell bound. LOL!

This black and white approach doesn't leave room for clear understanding, and many well-meaning Christians find themselves entangled in relationships with people that are detrimental to one's purpose.

So take a deep breath with me and let's look at sex from an energy standpoint. We know that sex is creative. Not only does it create babies, but it creates and nurtures a connection between two people. Sounds great, huh? Well it can be when both people are energetically healthy, have a similar level of consciousness, and neither operates at a lower vibration.

This umbilical cord like connection is called an energetic cord. These cords allow an exchange of energy between two people even after the act of sex is complete. You just can't walk away from a cord. It takes time and intentionality. It really is more than physical. Some Christian circles call this cord a "soul tie". Call it what you want, just know that sex creates intense bonds that can't be seen with the physical eye.

Are you still with me?

If you are, consider three energetic connections that can be detrimental to you and can take considerable time to sever the ties created. Any relationship that is detrimental to you is detrimental to your purpose. The time spent recovering from detrimental relationships delays you on your path to purpose and prevents you from executing vision at an optimal level.

1. Your partner operates at a lower vibration.

If you are a high vibrating being (which has a lot to do with your spiritual practice and the principles you live by), and you consistently engage with someone of a lower vibration intimately, your vibration will be impacted. Energy is exchanged in the sexual act. It can be that they benefit from your positive energy by taking yours on as their own or you could begin taking on their energy. If both partners are not operating at the same level, one is sure to lose and the other gains. It can be detrimental if your partner is operating at a drastically lower vibration than you.

If you are dealing with a partner who thrives in darkness such as manipulation or witchcraft, you will be impacted. If you are spiritually healthy or maintain a consistent honest relationship with your spiritual mentors, things of this nature can be detected. If you are living through the lens of past trauma, you can easily end up in an energetically draining relationship. Unhealed trauma has a way of making us overlook behaviors in others that are harmful to us. We are more susceptible to manipulation and being dominated when we have open wounds.

Christians love to talk about our gates, the ways, and places we take in things. For example, our ear gates and our eye gates. If you want to quickly transmit something from one person to another energetically, it can happen in the sexual act. So be careful.

Everyone does not deserve intimate access to you. I've seen many lives sidetracked simply from choosing the wrong partner. My father told me something profound as a teenager. His words were, "If you mess with trash, it will get in your eyes." I applied it in relationships. You can spend months and even years detaching from draining relationships. Any relationship that drains you physically is also draining some other area of your life. That could be your emotions, your bank account, or even your network. While we are in a sexual freedom era, to operate in such freedom without exposing the potential downside is negligent. The moral compass and spiritual consciousness of your partner does matter when you have a vision for your life.

2. You have multiple partners.

This scenario applies when you choose multiple sex partners. The whole concept sounds great for some. I offer no judgement. However, we should be honest. Sex is an intimate act. If the rules from scenario #1 apply, then you are spiritually going through life with multiple energy cords. Depending on the spiritual health of your partners, you can be on a slippery slope. Are you capable of carrying your energy and the energy of multiple people? I've seen this expressed as people feeling unstable and indecisive.

3. You have a single partner who has multiple partners.

You're in a relationship with one partner, but they have multiple partners. Again, I offer no judgement. This situation can happen with or without your awareness. I personally believe partners should be honest with each other in this area so that everyone knows how to protect themselves physically, emotionally, and spiritually.

The issue presented here is that your partner is bringing the energy of others to you in the sexual act. The cord from your partner is going in multiple directions and therefore can't be as strong with you. This is often reflected in the relationship in other ways. If you are an energy sensitive person, you can feel energy that is not your own and energy that is not that of your partner. It's your choice on how to proceed. Multiple foreign energies are being brought to your energy body and relationship. You may not get a physical glimpse of the person whose energy is being brought to you, but at a spiritual level, you can sense the energy.

We all have choices on how we choose to engage sexually, but we must honor the concept of taking on the energy of others. If we find ourselves not being able to focus on our purpose or vision, we should not overlook our sex life. Do not overlook the spiritual and emotional health of sex partners. There is more at stake in intimacy than STD transmission and pro-creation. The wrong relationships can pull us off course. The time and energy recovering thwarts our purpose.

Consider this: In your relationships do you typically embody a more submissive role? Do you naturally float to the background and devote a great deal of energy to your partner and their path? If you do, be careful of the character and direction of your chosen partners. By direction, I mean where exactly are they headed in life? Do they know? By character, I mean what spiritual principles do they strive towards? If you are naturally submissive and devoted to the path of your partner, be sure they carry the same set of values and consciousness as you. If not, they can carry your life down a non-purposeful path. It can easily turn into a domineering or abusive relationship. Power dynamics are at play in all relationships.

As women continue evolve and embrace their own power and their own agency, they naturally access all systems that impact them. Many women are critically examining the system of marriage. This relational transaction that is presented to us as necessary and good for us many times is not good to us. Marriage when defined by systems of patriarchy inherently places a lower value on the agency of women and her role in the relationship. Until we begin to view marriage as what Gary Zukav calls a "spiritual partnership", it will never fully honor women. Women will always get the short end of the stick. In our own agency, we can make the decision to forfeit marriage while exercising our own sexual freedom. In doing so, we must remember the energetic impacts of the partners that we choose to engage on this sacred level.

Hopefully, this chapter caused you to consider areas that may be overlooked in spiritual discussions. Living in a culture that privileges marriage can leave those who choose to remain single void of understanding. We can't simply ignore this topic. Our lives and purpose are at stake.

Assessing Your Partner(s)

Consider your life. Consider your sexual partner(s). Answer the questions below. Afterwards, engage your accountability partner to gain their perspective. Your accountability partner in this exercise should not be a sexual partner. *Note: Be open. Do not allow your emotions to prevent you from hearing someone else's perspective of your partner's impact on you.*

1. List the name of your partner(s):

2. Has your life stayed on course since engaging with them? Are you accomplishing the goals you set for yourself before you became involved with them?

3. Have you taken on their behaviors, their focus, and their purpose as your own? Be honest.

4. Are you constantly energetically and emotionally drained?

5. Are they supportive of your purpose and goals?

6

Live Until You Die

I originally preached this chapter as a sermon on January 26, 2020. Approximately 2 hours after we left the sanctuary, the headlines were full of the news of the tragic helicopter crash that claimed the life of Kobe Bryant and his beautiful daughter, Gianna. The text messages started rolling in from congregants in their shock, remembering the words I spoke earlier in the day. I often wonder what was left on Kobe's list of things he wanted to accomplish. We saw him at the highs and lows of his life. He released "Mamba Mentality" in 2018. This book entailed how his lifelong passion for basketball combined with discipline and dedication allowed him to soar and reach levels many will never see in their purpose. What else was in store? A catastrophic moment robbed us of hearing this from him.

As you read this chapter, consider the span of your life. Consider the grace of time God has allotted you on this earth. Whether you are rich, poor, smart, slow, or fast, one thing is certain. You will die. It's not if you will die, but when.

While the life of the biblical character David could have been deemed scandalous, the writer of the Acts 13:36 summed up his life this way:

"For David, after he had served the purpose of God in his own generation, fell asleep and was buried among his fathers and experienced decay [in the grave];"

David in all his majesty. One whose name was carried down through the Jewish faith. According to biblical writers, it was through his lineage which the promised Messiah came. Just like every other mortal will do, David died. But before he died, the writer says he did something.

"After <u>he had served the purpose of God</u> in his own generation, David fell asleep…"

He met eternity only after serving the purpose of God in his own generation. When your life has ended, could your name fit in this blank.

Try it here. Put your name in the blank. For after he/she had served the purpose of God in his/her own generation, _____ fell asleep and was buried among his/her ancestors.

Like David, there is a purpose of God in YOU for this generation. And you have specific assignments in this lifetime that are meant to be completed.

For this reason, we must LIVE until we die. Until death comes, our purpose must be at the forefront of our lives. We won't get do-overs.

So many of us believe we have 60 and 70 years to live. I certainly don't want to sound morbid, but we really don't know long we are allotted this life. There are windows of opportunity right here in this new year, so write that book, pursue that grant, start that business, or finish that degree.

There are seasons in life. There are times when the fruit manifests quickly and other times there is drought. We don't know how long we are allotted this particular season of life.

Often, we get distracted by things that have no correlation to our purpose. This causes us to miss seasons that are fruitful. By fruitful, I mean seasons where the manifestation of the seed is quick. We miss those seasons because we are not all in and have too many distractions in the frame of our lives.

This year is a fruitful season – so be all in. We must live until we die and as long as we live, live on PURPOSE!

When we consider the life of Jesus, it seems like he was all over the place. We read stories where he was going from here to there and to everywhere. He was all over Galilee. His travels were necessary to his purpose.

Consider Luke 4:42-43:

[42] When daybreak came, Jesus left [Simon Peter's house] and went to a secluded place; and the crowds were searching for Him, and [they] came to Him and tried to keep Him from leaving them. 43 But He said, "I must preach [the good news of] the kingdom of God to the other cities also because I was sent for this purpose."

Jesus had 33 good years. What if he had spent them distracted? What if he had spent them being in the places where everyone else wanted him to be? What if he tried to be what everyone else wanted him to be? Jesus clearly denies their request for him to stay and cites his purpose as his reason for leaving.

Like Jesus, when we truly serve our generation, we impact the generations to come. The greater our surrender to purpose, the greater God can work through us. All God is asking is to let God be God in us. The greater God can move through us the greater our vibration will rise.

In life, it's not just one surrender, we must surrender to every breadcrumb along the way. At certain spots on our journey — we'll get more revelation regarding what God requires of us.

God is wise. God knows God's creation. If God were to show us our ending, we couldn't handle it. If the Divine were to show us our full capacity at once, many of us would shrink and go back to our little hiding places. Perhaps even living a life of no value to anyone, not even ourselves.

'Tis the season to be in full throttle. It is not the time for braking and questioning the things surrounding our purpose that we've already confirmed as true. It is time to manifest purpose in our own lives.

It's not the season to take detours because whatever we do in this season will have long lasting impacts. If we decide to go down a path we know is not purposeful for us, we have to be prepared to make our stay. We will be there for a while.

Lighten Your Load

The writer of Hebrews 12 describes how we can run our race efficiently.

"<u>Stripping off</u> every unnecessary weight and the sin which so easily *and* cleverly entangles us, let us <u>run</u> with <u>endurance</u> and active <u>persistence</u> the race that is set before us."

Most of us are clear on sin, but let's talk about weights. Weights are anything that impede or hinder us on our journey. We can become comfortable with our weights. Some overlooked weights are brokenness, trauma, and behaviors that prevent us from being in an optimal state. These weights are in our blind spots that everyone else sees but us. Weights prevents us from living on purpose because they stand between us and that next breadcrumb.

What's standing between you and the next breadcrumb?

What's keeping you from picking it up?

That's the weight I want you to consider.

Is it fear?

Is it a relationship that has run its course?

Is it an addiction that you keep hidden?

Lay aside EVERY weight that entangles you.

When I was a kid, before CD's, there were cassette tapes. If somehow the ribbon in the cassette got tangled up, it took a lot of time and energy untangling it. I remember using a pencil for hours trying to get one of my favorite cassettes back on track. Until the ribbon was aligned perfectly, the cassette was not useful.

Weights entangle us that way. We exhaust unnecessary time and energy untangling ourselves from situations brought on by weights. We can't have maximum impact in life until we lay them aside. We will never be efficient attempting to execute in purpose with weights slowing us down or causing us to trip and fall.

A Hidden Agenda

What if I told you that your soul has a hidden agenda? It has a hidden motive: to bring about in you exactly what God created you to be.

You have to consciously agree with your soul. You have to align with your soul. You have to yield all of your being and allow God to unfold within you.

Digging Deeper

Consider each question below. Review your answers with your accountability partner. Listen for their perspective.

1. What's standing between you and the next breadcrumb?

a. Who can you trust to tell about this "weight"?

2. In what spaces in your life in this season do you feel God has assigned you? For what reason?

3. Name two people in your life you believe are living out their life's purpose? What characteristics have you observed that made you draw this conclusion?

7

Breadcrumbs in Today's World

As I complete this manuscript, we are halfway through 2020. A project that started before COVID-19 ravished the world is pushing through the birth canal. Before it could be delivered, the entire world was collectively reminded of the necessity of social change. Massive protests broke out all over the world after the murder of Mr. George Floyd and others.

The first half of 2020 was definitely a season where purpose carried me. Many times I came back to my own manuscript for guidance and direction. Allowing Spirit to work through me on this project gave me focus. Every suggestion in this book has been challenged by 2020.

If you're reading this, celebrate that you are surviving in a pandemic. Actually, you are surviving in two pandemics. One, being COVID-19. Two, being the racial injustice that is still prevalent today. I want to encourage you to not only survive, but thrive. Thriving amidst two pandemics will require you to live purposely. While we witness the formation of a drastically different physical world, we must acknowledge a spiritual awakening is taking place as we are forced to confront ourselves.

Ultimately, I knew Breadcrumbs to Purpose was "pandemic work" for me. As COVID-19 carried out its mission assigned by its creators, my mission was to birth this book. With any mission, opposition comes. The greatest opposition for me came in the form of distractions that would attempt to rob me of my joy and my mental clarity. As I lived in a tiny apartment alone, it became increasingly difficult to hear my own voice as the fear of the unknown and isolation attempted to overtake my being.

I quickly learned that as a black woman, I rightly desired to understand my role in the fight for social change. In my role as a podcaster and community organizer, I received so many external tugs. I followed my passion for my brothers and sisters on the front lines of protests to engage me in my work as an organizer. That was necessary for my expression.

As time progressed, I found my mental and spiritual stability and Spirit whispered to me repeatedly, "Finish the book". My pandemic work was this book. My role during COVID-19: "Finish the book". While protestors raise their voice all over the country for Ahmaud Arbery, Breonna Taylor, and George Floyd, my role was "Finish the book".

Both pandemics are forcing us as spiritual beings to focus only on the external. COVID-19 is forcing us to give great detail to our physical bodies. We are giving attention to wearing masks, how we feel, and how far away we are from others. We are stimulated by a news cycle that focuses on the death rate instead of the survival rate. The fight for equality of black and brown folks around the globe forces many of us into the reality of accessing our skin color, what others think of us, and a constant fight or flight mode ensues. We have been forced to deal with our physical realities, and for black folks this has been magnified in 2020 by the presence of two pandemics.

Many of us have been in survival mode, but God desires that we thrive. When there is not a careful balance between internal and external focus, we lose our power. True power is sourced from within. True power comes from our connection to Source. There are moments in our lives where we must lay down the external world and be fueled by our internal world.

My thriving has required me to take moments to lay down my role as pastor, my black womanhood, and my community organizing to go within. Spirit empowers us to do the work we've been called to do in our external world and understands the complexities of our identity. As I laid down my responsibilities and identity in the external world, I could hear clearly and be centered again. Thereby gaining the clarity and the strength to continue.

As we started this journey, I asserted that purpose was an internal discovery which allows life to unfold before us. I want to reemphasize that fact. Don't allow external stimulations to act make us forget our internal reality. Don't allow external tugs make us head down paths that lead to nowhere. Don't be found busy, doing nothing.

I encourage you to live each day with an overall theme in mind. That theme should be derived from purpose. It should be sourced by purpose and not the news cycle. It should be sourced by purpose, not by fear.

Remember, if we are consistently at a high frequency vibration, many things will come in our direction. We are in essence a magnet when in this state. However, drawing is not the end game. The universe has done its job by sending. It is our duty to decipher what is aligned with who we are and why we are here. As many paths unfold, be sure to choose the path of purpose. How will we recognize it? Follow the breadcrumbs. They will surely take us home.

It has been an honor to journey with you. I'm grateful you allowed me to share space with you. As I step off your path, I pray you feel the warmth beaming down. I sense that your way is a little brighter and your load is a little lighter. Not just because of me, but because you made the choice to "stand in the sun" with me. The only person sanctioned to introduce something new into the narrative of your life is YOU. As I release your hand and you continue down the path, may you take charge of your life and don't let life have charge of you. Live on purpose!

Before You Go

I offer gratitude for sharing this journey with you. If *Breadcrumbs to Purpose* has reaffirmed or increased your awareness around your Divinely assigned purpose, please share your story on Amazon.com. Your story will help others on their journey towards purpose.

Keep up with me at www.EvaMelton.com. Feel free to shoot me an email at evaRmelton@gmail.com to engage in further dialogue. I would love to connect with you on Facebook, Twitter or Instagram.

Standing in The Sun,

Eva R. Melton

September 2020

www.ingramcontent.com/pod-product-compliance
Lightning Source LLC
Chambersburg PA
CBHW070209100426
42743CB00013B/3113